A Lamb on a Limb

by Jan Stewart
illustrated by Pat Lucas-Morris

Core Decodable 85

McGraw Hill Education

Bothell, WA • Chicago, IL • Columbus, OH • New York, NY

MHEonline.com

Send all inquiries to:
McGraw-Hill Education
8787 Orion Place
Columbus, OH 43240

ISBN: 978-0-02-144887-6
MHID: 0-02-144887-6

Printed in the United States of America.

8 9 10 11 12 LCR 27 26 25 24 23

Is that Sam's stuffed lamb?

Yes! It is his lamb on that limb.

We can get Sam's lamb off the limb!
Let's think of a plan.

Can we grab the lamb with a thumb?
Can thumbs get Sam's lamb?

I have crumbs from my sandwich.
Crumbs are no help to get Sam's lamb.

Thumbs and crumbs did not get Sam's lamb.
Sam's lamb is still on a limb.

Dad can get Sam's lamb off the limb.
He did not even have to climb the tree!